From Wandering to Walking

A Testimony of God's Love

Alex Horton

i

ISBN: 979-8-9934894-0-7

Printed in the United States of America.

For everyone still wandering

Table of Contents

Introduction

I used to look up at the moon, imagining that vast distance. I would imagine what a small speck I would be from its surface, and wonder about the universe. I would think of my problems, and how meaningless they were, because who am I? I would sit there, thinking that I'm nothing more than a cosmic coincidence, and I would go inside and go to sleep. Lately, I've been looking at the moon. I don't think about how small I am, and how little I mean. Instead, I think of how much time and effort God put into creating me. I think about how I was designed specially for Him. I look at the moon now and see the beauty that God put on this earth for us to bear witness to, a reflection of His majesty and His care.

Before I found my faith, life didn't have much meaning to it. I had to search everywhere to find meaning. At times, I thought that serving others with everything I had was a way to find meaning. At another time, I thought that I could find meaning if I isolated myself from others and tried to just live my life the way I wanted to. I was always searching for something; whether that be love, meaning, or joy. I had a lot of questions about identity and who I was. I never really found a good answer. I was always indecisive and never knew what I was going to do with my life. Looking up at the moon, I saw something so much bigger than myself, and it made me feel tiny. It took away my worries but instead replaced them with shame for thinking that my problems were so great, when others had circumstances far worse than my own.

God was always working in the wings for me. I never really saw quite what He was doing, but looking back, I see some of the work that He did. The main thing I think of was putting a friend in my path who questioned my faith. They asked me what I believed, and I wasn't sure. I started really paying attention at church and trying to figure out what they were trying to tell me. Sometimes this worked well, other times it didn't. Now, while that was a good steppingstone, I unfortunately did lose my faith for a while after about a year. Later, I was exploring my faith in the form of devotionals and sermons. I wanted to teach others what I also didn't know for a long time, even when I didn't fully understand it.

It was while I was writing one of these that it all clicked for me. I was sitting down, writing, and read a verse for one of the points I was going to make. Romans 5:8 "But God demonstrates His love for us in this: that while we were still sinners Christ died for us." I sat back after reading that, and understood what God's love really is. God created us out of love. He designed each and every one of us out of love for us. He sent a Son, sinless, to die for us, so that we could be saved. I had to take a minute to process that. I knew that my family loved me, I knew that I had people surrounding me who loved me in one form or another, but I realized that God's love is so much more than humans could ever give. I realized in that moment that even at my lowest, Christ knew me and loved me. I was never meaningless; I was just lost.

This book is a testimony of my own faith. I know that it may not be the same for everyone, but I hope to inspire others to find faith in God. I will be clear: I am broken, as we all are. Nobody is perfect. However, I will never stop saying that we are all loved by the God who created each of us. This book is a testimony of my life, and my faith, but it's also (I hope) an inspiration to all those who feel lost, or broken, or unworthy of love or saving. If you get nothing else from this book, understand this: you are loved. You are worthy. God will always open His arms to you.

This book is an invitation as well. For everybody, whether you're a long-time believer, a new believer, or unsure about any faith at all. I invite you to read this testimony and reflect on what it is that God may be saying to you. How does the book make you feel? In my eyes, if I only bring one person closer to God through this book, then I have succeeded. We may not be able to change the whole world, but if we impact one person's life, their entire world has changed.

This is an open invitation for you, or anyone you may feel called to share this with, to join me through this walk. This book is not perfect, but neither is my life. I make a lot of mistakes and always will. The only thing we can do is move forward and forgive ourselves, as we are forgiven by He who is perfect. The moon no longer symbolizes emptiness or how small or worthless I am.

Instead, I look to the moon and see the beauty that God created,

and I'm reminded that the same hands who created that beautiful

moon also created me. I am no less beautiful, no less intentional,

and no less seen than the moon, because I am created in the image

of God. His love meets us wherever we are, even when we wander

away from Him, and He will always call us back to walk alongside

Him.

Chapter 1 – Beneath the Moonlight

I used to lie awake at night, the moon illuminating the room as thoughts raced through my mind, wondering what my life would be. The only things I could hear were the crickets outside, the hum of the fan, and the sounds of my racing thoughts. I had so many ideas of what I could do with my life, whether it be working in law enforcement, or in a tech field, or even as an author. I wanted to become a police officer, ensuring safety of others. I wanted to be someone that was called to assist and protect. I could train in a specialized field, particularly SWAT marksman. I wanted to be someone that was needed, and someone who could protect those who couldn't protect themselves. I loved the thought of the responsibility of upholding order. The weight of the uniform on me, and the weight of all that would think of me. I wondered if I was strong enough, mentally or physically, to accept that role in my life.

I wanted to work in tech because I love working with rules and regulations of how things work. I could sit in front of a problem and know that there is a set solution. I also wanted to do it because my grandma was plagued by hackers or scammers trying to steal her information. I wanted to protect her, and others like her. I love the thought of fixing something for someone else. I want to see their eyes light up as a problem is solved. I was also terribly frustrated with the knowledge that people exploit others who don't know better to steal from them. I wanted to be an author to tell stories that people would fall in love with. I could imagine my name on the cover of a book, and I felt pride well up in my chest. I wanted to write something that I could be proud of. I wanted my audience to love the characters as much as I did, and to grow with the world that was built on the pages.

I never really knew, and I would bounce between all of these. I would think about my life and I could see where I was. I could think about what I would have to do for my life to go in a good direction, but I could see about 3 months into the future plans that I had, and then I couldn't see anything else. It was like a book, the beginning written, the end written, but the middle was blank. It scared me, because I had no control over that. I couldn't see a future with myself, let alone a partner that I could love. I would look around and see others with partners, kids, houses, and plans for their lives, and I would wonder what was wrong with me. All these dreams filled my head, but none of them filled my heart. No matter which path I imagined, I couldn't shake the feeling that something was missing.

As much as I dreamed of the future, the present only left me feeling empty. No matter where I turned, I couldn't find a lasting sense of purpose. I searched for it in the people I surrounded myself with, in the work I took on, and even in the dreams I clung to at night, but nothing filled the hollow space inside me. Everything I tried slipped through my fingers like water.

Video games became one of my most familiar escapes. I could sit in front of a glowing screen for hours, disappearing into worlds where there was always something to do: a quest to complete, a battle to fight, a goal to reach. In those digital spaces I felt a fleeting sense of direction, like I was part of something bigger. There were clear rules, measurable progress, and the safety of knowing I could always start over if I failed. For a while it dulled the restless thoughts that haunted me at night. But the glow of the screen would eventually fade, and I would be left sitting in the same quiet room, the same questions pressing in around me: Who am I? What am I here for?

When the games lost their hold, I turned to people to fill the emptiness. I chased friendships and relationships, hoping they would give me a sense of belonging and value. I fell into circles that weren't good for me, and relationships that were toxic and led me down paths I wish I had never walked. I became someone who needed to feel loved by others in order to feel like I had worth at all. If someone liked me, I was happy; if they pulled away, I felt like I had failed. I started changing who I was to fit in with whoever I was around, adjusting my words, my interests, and even my personality to match theirs.

Looking back now, I can see how much of myself I was losing. At the time, though, it felt like survival; like maybe if I could just find the right person, the right friend group, the right environment, then I would finally feel whole. But every attempt ended the same way, leaving me emptier than before. I was learning how to look for love from others, but I had never learned how to love myself, and no one else could do that for me.

I was confused, and nothing in my life seemed to make sense. My worth rose and fell with the opinions of others, and I let their approval or rejection define me. If someone liked me, I felt happy and secure. If they didn't, I spiraled into sadness, convinced something was wrong with me, and I would do whatever I could to change myself to fit their expectations. I called myself a chameleon, because I had learned to blend in with whoever I was around.

With one group of friends, I would act louder and more reckless, laughing at jokes I didn't find funny just to belong. With another, I would soften my voice, pretend to share their interests, and nod along so I wouldn't stand out. At school, I wore one face. At home, I wore another. With friends, another still. I became so used to slipping into whatever role I thought people wanted from me that I lost track of the person I truly was.

At first, I told myself it was harmless. Everyone changes a little depending on who they are with, right? But over time, the weight of the masks grew heavy. I began to realize that in trying to be everything for everyone else, I was becoming nothing for myself. I could not tell where the act ended and the real me began. I had worn so many different faces for so long that the one that really belonged to me had faded into the background, almost beyond recognition.

Deep down, I knew it was dishonest; not only to others, but to myself. Yet I kept doing it, because being wanted, even for a false version of myself, felt better than being invisible. Still, the cost was steep. Every mask I put on pushed me further from knowing who I was created to be. I was living as fragments of borrowed identities, while my true identity remained hidden, and with each passing day I felt more lost than before.

Over time, I managed to find my way back to something that looked almost normal. The chaos inside had not disappeared, but I was learning to steady myself enough to pass as someone who had it all together. I surrounded myself with better people than before, people who treated me with kindness and respect instead of pulling me into toxic cycles. That shift mattered more than I realized at the time. It gave me the space to breathe again, even if I still was not sure who I was.

One of the biggest turning points was when I began attending a youth group. At first, it was just another place to be, a safe environment that kept me occupied. I did not know what to expect. But when I walked in, I immediately noticed something different about the people there. They were not trying to tear me down, and they were not asking me to perform to be accepted. They were simply kind. There was laughter, warmth, and a sense of belonging that I had not felt in a long time.

Still, I did not let my guard down easily. I had been hurt before, and I was not willing to risk that again. I kept everyone at arm's length, showing them only what I wanted them to see. On the outside, I wore the mask of someone who was happy, calm, and steady. I smiled when they smiled, I joined in their activities, and I gave just enough of myself to blend in. But on the inside, I was still a whirlwind of conflicting emotions: doubt, fear, loneliness, and the constant ache of searching for meaning.

Even so, something about that place kept pulling me back. Week after week, I returned. At first, I thought it was just routine, another place to pass the time. But it became clear there was something deeper going on. For the first time in a long time, I felt seen. Not in the way I felt when I was trying to prove myself or earn someone's attention, but in a quieter and gentler way. Being in that group gave me a calm I could not find anywhere else.

I wrestled with the question of whether they were accepting me for who I really was, or simply for the version of myself I presented. Part of me was afraid to find out the answer. What if they only loved the mask and not the person underneath? That fear kept me silent. I did not pry, I did not push, and I did not try to reveal too much. But deep down, I longed for it to be real. I wanted to believe that maybe, just maybe, there was a place where I did not have to be anyone other than myself.

Looking back now, I can see the grace of God in that season. Even though I had not yet discovered the depth of His love for me, He was already weaving it into my story through people who showed me kindness. The youth group became a kind of lifeline, not because I suddenly had everything figured out, but because I realized I did not have to face my confusion alone. It was the first taste of acceptance that felt different, the first crack in the wall I had built around myself. Even though I could not name it then, I was beginning to see the shadow of God's hand at work in my life.

In hindsight, I see that all the places I searched for meaning were like broken wells. They looked solid from the outside, but when I reached in, they could not hold water. I poured myself into serving others, isolating myself, and chasing after different ideas of who I thought I should be, but none of it lasted. The emptiness always came back, no matter how much effort I gave. At the time, I believed that was simply how life worked. I thought nothing could truly satisfy me, so I settled for temporary comforts and convinced myself they were enough.

Much later, I came to understand that God had already spoken to this kind of wandering. In Jeremiah 2:13 He says, "My people have committed two sins: They have forsaken me, the spring of living water, and have dug their own cisterns, broken cisterns that cannot hold water." That verse struck me with unusual clarity. It described exactly what I had been doing. I had turned away from the spring of living water without even knowing it, and in its place I dug wells that were cracked and dry. I drank from them, desperate for satisfaction, but they could never quench my thirst.

For me, those broken wells showed up in distractions, in relationships, and in the masks I wore to feel accepted. But broken wells are not unique to me. They can take countless forms. Some people bury themselves in work, convinced that the next promotion will finally bring peace. Others run after possessions, filling their houses with more and more, only to find that nothing new can calm the ache in their soul. Some chase after love in all the wrong places, hoping that another person can heal their loneliness. Others numb themselves with entertainment, substances, or busyness, afraid of what the silence might reveal.

The details change from one life to another, but the result is always the same. None of those things can hold water. None of them can satisfy the deep thirst of the soul. I thought I was different, that if I tried hard enough one of my wells would work. If I could only be successful, if I could only be loved, if I could only be important to someone, then I would finally feel whole. But every attempt ended the same way, leaving me drier than before. The harder I worked at filling myself, the more the cracks in my wells widened.

Jeremiah's image is so clear. On one side there is a spring, flowing and alive, with fresh water that never runs out. On the other side are broken cisterns, cracked containers that spoil what little is poured in. One is life-giving. The other promises much but delivers nothing. Yet how often we choose the cistern over the spring, convinced that our own way will be enough. That was my story for so long. I had access to God's love, but I kept turning back to my own fragile solutions.

When I think of it now, I realize the thirst itself was not the problem. The thirst was a sign. It was a reminder that I was made for something more. My soul was crying out for the living water that only God gives. The tragedy was not that I was thirsty, but that I kept going to places that could never satisfy me.

Perhaps you know that feeling too. Maybe you have chased after your own wells, hoping they would be enough, only to find them dry. Maybe you have reached for success, approval, or comfort, only to discover that none of them could hold the weight of your longing. If so, you are not alone. I know what that emptiness feels like, and I know the shame of trying to fill it in all the wrong ways. But here is the good news: God does not leave us stranded at broken wells. He does not condemn us for our wandering. Instead, He invites us back to the spring, where His living water flows freely for anyone who is thirsty.

That is where my story began to shift. The wells I dug for myself were empty, but the spring of living water was waiting for me all along. I did not yet understand the fullness of it, but I was on the edge of discovering that God's love is greater than my wandering. Even when I turned to emptiness, He was patiently calling me to come and drink. I did not know it then, but I was standing on the edge of the verse that would change everything for me.

Chapter 2 – Struggles and Brokenness

Through my life, I have experienced a lot of hardship. From struggles with family dynamics, to battles with mental health, to doubts about who I am or what I am doing, and even failures in my actions, brokenness has been a recurring part of my story. At the time, I thought those struggles defined me. Now I see that they were the very places where God would later meet me.

I have briefly talked before about how I was not the best son in the world. I habitually lied, tried to hide things, and avoided responsibility whenever I could. I stayed up late, ignored what I was told, and at times was openly disrespectful to my mom. With her being the only parent in the picture, every conflict between us felt magnified. The house carried the weight of unspoken tension. There was never really a resolution when we fought. Instead, time would slowly take the sharp edge off the anger until we could both act as if nothing had happened. But it always came back. I found myself butting heads with her constantly, whether it was about how I spent my free time, the kind of work I did, or the people I chose to be in relationships with.

In many ways, I was grateful to leave home and join the military. It felt like an escape, a chance to start over and get out of the cycle of conflict that I had helped create. Walking away was freeing, but it was also frightening. Later, I would realize that it had been a rushed decision, a young man trying to solve years of tension in one bold move. I wanted to believe I was taking control, but in truth, I was still running.

The military was not what I thought it would be. I was only in for about eight months before I left due to mental health struggles. Basic training is designed to break down the individual and rebuild them into part of a unit. For someone like me, who already felt like an outcast, that process was brutal. I could never quite fit in, and the more the days went on, the more I felt out of place. There were moments when I tried to be strong, but I did not know how. I tried to wear a smile, to act like everything was fine, but I could not pretend forever. There were nights when I cried myself to sleep, the weight of exhaustion and fear pressing in on me.

During that time, something traumatic happened to me. It left me unable to sleep well, constantly hyper-vigilant, always looking over my shoulder even during training. When you are already running on very little rest, broken sleep does not sustain you. It leaves you raw, shaky, and barely functioning. My mistakes began piling up. I started to wonder if what had happened to me was somehow my fault, and if I would ever make it through to the end of boot camp.

In the end, I did report what happened. It was one of the hardest things I have ever done. I was scared of retaliation, scared of judgment, scared that others would think less of me. Yet at the same time, I felt proud of myself. There was a small measure of relief in telling the truth, though it came mixed with a new fear of how others would see me. That fear never fully went away, but I knew I had done what I needed to do.

Later, in my military career, things did not get easier. I had a roommate who showed no respect for my need for sleep, leaving me running on maybe four hours a night if I was lucky. Then came the moment that finally broke me. I woke up one night to find him watching me sleep. That image is burned in my memory. This time I did not hesitate. I reported him immediately, and I was transferred to a different room. But the damage was already done. That incident pushed me into the downward spiral that eventually landed me in the hospital for mental health and led to my discharge.

When I left, it felt like failure. I wondered if I had wasted my chance, if my struggle meant I was not strong enough. At the same time, I knew I had made it out with my life, and that was something to hold on to. It was not the ending I wanted, but it was a new beginning, even if I could not see it clearly at the time.

Afterward, I tried to rebuild. I worked as a security guard, and for a time, I enjoyed the work. There was something steady about it, something that reminded me of my earlier dream of being a police officer. I worked nights, evenings, and days, shifting between schedules, and found satisfaction in the routine. But as much as I liked the work, I wanted more. I wanted a degree. I wanted to prove that I could move forward.

That desire led me into cybersecurity. At first, it seemed like the perfect fit. I got certifications, dove into the material, and even started my degree in the field. The work gave me purpose for a while. I thought of my grandma, how she had been plagued by scammers and hackers trying to take advantage of her, and I felt motivated to protect people like her. For a short time, that made me proud. But the deeper I went, the more I felt something was missing. Sitting in front of a screen, following rules and solving puzzles, left me empty. I did not feel like I was making the impact I longed for. I was learning, achieving, and even succeeding, but the drive to make a lasting change in the world was gone.

One of my deepest failures, though, was not in work or the military but in a relationship with someone I once deeply cared for. At that point in my life, I was not strong in my faith, and I entered into the relationship without the right foundation. She encouraged me to grow in faith, and for a while, I did. But it was shallow. I was living out faith for her, not for myself. I wanted her approval more than I wanted God's presence.

I started lying about how I spent my free time. I would do things she would not have agreed with, and then tell her I was doing something else. Each lie piled guilt on my shoulders, but I pushed it down, unwilling to face the shame of admitting the truth. We stopped communicating in a healthy way. I disrespected her, betrayed her trust, and avoided the conversations that could have healed us. When the relationship eventually fell apart, I told myself it was not my fault. I blamed her, I blamed circumstances, I blamed anyone but myself. Only later did I face the truth: I had failed. I had not respected her, and I had not shown her the love she deserved. In time, I came to realize something even harder. I could not truly love her, because I had never learned to love myself or to rest in the love of Christ.

During a lot of those years, I escaped through distractions. Video games, movies, pouring myself into people, throwing myself into work; anything to avoid the reality of my brokenness.

Games gave me a rush. I loved shooter games, or vast open worlds like Skyrim. They gave me quests, goals, a sense of direction. For a while, they filled the hollow space inside me. Victory felt good. But eventually, the rewards grew smaller, the challenges harder, and the satisfaction faded. The hero on the screen was no longer enough, and neither was I.

Movies and TV shows were no different. I would sit down, lose myself in story after story, and when the credits rolled, the day was gone. Sometimes I would watch until the sun had set, realizing I had done nothing. The guilt came heavy. I would try to mimic the characters I admired, chasing after impossible standards, and every failure pushed me deeper into shame and depression.

When games and movies lost their power, I poured myself into people. On the surface, it looked like selflessness, but it came at the cost of my own well-being. I wanted people to like me, so I gave and gave without caring for myself. I saw myself as less valuable than others, so I believed their needs mattered more than mine. It left me drained and burnt out, unable to keep going.

The same pattern showed up in work. I would throw myself into my job, taking on extra shifts, staying late, and helping others without question. I once worked sixteen hours straight just so I would not have to lie awake with my thoughts. Staying busy made me feel important, but in reality, it was only another escape. I wanted everyone to think I was amazing, that I was unshakable, that I was perfect. The truth was the opposite. Nobody is perfect. We are all broken.

It was in that brokenness that God began to meet me. When I took the time to reflect on my life, I realized something simple but powerful. I was not perfect. I never had been. But God did not demand perfection. He only asked for obedience and loyalty.

Scripture confirmed what I was beginning to understand. Romans 3:23 says, "For all have sinned and fall short of the glory of God." At first, those words could have felt condemning. Instead, they felt like comfort. I realized that I did not have to be perfect, because I could not be. None of us can. My failures were not unique, they were part of being human.

For the first time, I felt loved even in my imperfection. I felt comfort, knowing that God saw me as I was and still wanted me. I realized that while perfection was never attainable, drawing closer to God would bring me nearer to the only One who is perfect. That truth freed me from the crushing weight of trying to live up to impossible standards.

Once I admitted my brokenness, I could finally see it clearly. It was painful to name my failures, and even harder to admit them to others. There were things I could only bring to God, in prayer, because I was too ashamed to share them with anyone else. Yet the more I prayed, the more He helped me see. The process was slow and uncomfortable, and it will continue for the rest of my life. But it was necessary. Being broken is not only about living with sin, it is about being separated from God. If I had refused to admit my faults, I would have never built a real relationship with Him.

My brokenness was not wasted. God used every pain, every struggle, every failure to teach me humility, compassion, and patience. He even used my testimony, as raw and messy as it was, to encourage others who were walking through their own struggles. What I once thought disqualified me became a part of how God was shaping me.

Admitting that I needed Him did not mean He fixed everything that was broken. It meant He showed me what was still good. I will never be perfect, but I do not have to be. I am who God designed me to be, and His love is enough.

Chapter 3 – The Turning of the Heart

Through my life, like I said before, I tried countless things to escape from the darkness that troubled me. The problem was, those things could never bring me lasting joy. The video games would leave me with a sense of not being good enough. The movies would make me feel like I had wasted away for an entire day. Each escape dulled the pain for a moment, but once the distraction faded, I was left right where I started: restless and empty, wondering why nothing ever seemed to fill me completely. I thought if I just found the right hobby, the right person, or the right job, the ache would go away. But it never did. There was always that quiet question whispering in the back of my mind, "Is this really all there is?"

When I started going to that youth group, I didn't expect to find fulfillment. I was, truthfully, there for the pizza and games. It was something to do, a break from the routine of work and home. I liked being around people who smiled easily and seemed to have direction, even if I didn't share it. However, the more I went, the more I began to notice something that unsettled me. These people weren't just happy; they were content. It wasn't the shallow kind of joy that fades once the event ends. It was quieter and deeper, like a steady current beneath everything they did.

At first, I didn't know what to make of it. I would listen as they talked about their faith, about answered prayers or things that had happened in their lives that they gave God credit for. I nodded along, but inside I wondered why I couldn't have what they did. Why did they seem so at peace while I was still fighting myself? I didn't try to build that kind of faith for myself; I just compared. I told myself they must have had easier lives, better support, fewer mistakes to carry. I watched their joy from a distance and assumed it was something I wasn't meant to have.

When I would go home after youth group, I'd sit in my room and scroll through my phone, seeing people posting pictures of their perfect relationships, their new houses, their smiling families. I would ask what I was doing wrong. Why did I keep coming up short? I was trying, wasn't I? I worked hard. I tried to be kind. But nothing seemed to fall into place. It was a dangerous cycle of envy and shame, and the more I compared myself to others, the more broken I felt.

Over time, though, something began to shift. It wasn't loud or dramatic. It was slow, almost like a seed growing underground where I couldn't see it yet. The more I went to the group, the more questions I found myself asking, not about other people, but about myself and about God. I began wondering if maybe the problem wasn't that He wasn't there, but that I wasn't looking for Him in the right way. Questions like, "How could I find a connection with God?" and "Am I meant to be religious?" started to echo in my thoughts when everything else went quiet.

That was when I was invited to join the church's traditional choir. I didn't do it out of spiritual conviction; I did it because I love to sing. Music had always been one of the few things that brought me peace. When I sang, I felt like the noise in my head finally quieted down. It was a way to express something I couldn't always say out loud. So I joined, thinking it would be another way to pass time and enjoy what I loved. But something unexpected happened.

As I sang those old hymns, something stirred in me. I didn't fully understand the words then, but the melodies carried a weight I hadn't felt before. Lines like "Amazing grace, how sweet the sound" or "Be thou my vision" started to sink deeper each time I sang them. I wasn't just performing; I was beginning to feel. I realized that those songs weren't just music to the people around me; they were prayers. I saw how their faces changed when they sang, how their eyes softened, how peace seemed to settle over them. I didn't have that peace yet, but I wanted it.

Even after I grew too old for the youth group, the people there didn't forget me. They would check in, send messages, or ask how I was doing when they saw me around church. It wasn't forced or out of obligation; they genuinely cared. I wasn't used to that. In the past, people had drifted away once I wasn't useful to them. These people stayed, even when I didn't have much to offer. That kindness, simple as it was, began to chip away at my defenses. Over time, I started noticing that the people around me were changing too, or maybe it was that I was changing. The friends I kept were more godly, the conversations deeper, the laughter cleaner. The destructive influences that used to fill my life were fading away, replaced by people who encouraged growth instead of distraction.

Despite that progress, I still struggled. Anger and lust were two of my greatest battles. I would get frustrated and angry over small things, snapping without reason. I told myself I would do better next time, but when stress hit, I failed again. Lust was another struggle, one that filled me with shame because I knew it went against what I was trying to build. Even when I wanted to live rightly, temptation crept in. It was exhausting. Each failure made me question whether I could ever truly change.

Even in my attempts to be more faithful, I often missed the point. I would pray for things I wanted, like strength, success, clarity, or answers, but deep down, I still wanted life to go my way. I wasn't praying for God's will; I was praying for my comfort. I wanted His blessing without surrendering my control. When things didn't go how I hoped, I grew frustrated and confused. I would say, "God, why aren't You answering me?" But I wasn't listening for His answer.

Looking back, I see how patient He was with me. He didn't turn away from my selfish prayers; He used them to teach me. Over time, I realized that a relationship with God couldn't be one-sided. It required not only speaking but also listening. It required not only believing but also obeying. I had to stop living life on my own terms if I truly wanted to walk with Him.

A verse that captures that struggle perfectly is Jeremiah 29:13, which says, "You will seek me and find me when you seek me with all your heart." For so long, I had been seeking God with half my heart, the half that wanted comfort, not change. I thought I was searching for Him, but what I was really searching for was peace without surrender. And that kind of peace doesn't exist. I could not find God while holding on to my old ways.

When I finally stopped trying to live my life the way I wanted and began living in the way that God called me to, things started to change. It didn't happen overnight. It came through small realizations, a softer word when I would have spoken harshly, a moment of patience where I would have once lashed out, a prayer that shifted from "give me what I want" to "help me do what You want." The change wasn't loud, but it was real.

As I learned more about God, reading Scripture, listening to sermons, and reflecting on what faith really means, I began to see how He had been pursuing me all along. Even in the times I thought He was distant, He was right beside me. Every closed door, every failure, every ache was a redirection, not rejection. I began to understand that God doesn't stand back watching our lives like a spectator. He steps in, nudging us, guiding us, sometimes even allowing us to stumble so that we can learn to lean on Him.

When that realization hit me, I felt a spark of life I hadn't known before. It was like breathing fresh air after being underwater too long. The idea that the Creator of everything, the same God who hung the stars and shaped the mountains, wanted to know me personally was overwhelming. I had spent so much time chasing meaning in the world, but the One who made the world had been chasing me.

That understanding changed everything. I saw that all the moments I had labeled as failures were actually invitations. When I lost my way, He was showing me how much I needed Him. When I fell into anger, He was teaching me patience. When I wrestled with lust, He was reminding me that true love is rooted in holiness, not desire. When I prayed for my will to be done, He was patiently waiting for me to learn that His will is better.

There's something humbling about realizing that God never gave up on me, even when I had given up on myself. Every time I thought I was too far gone, too broken, too flawed, He met me with grace. The moment I started to seek Him with my whole heart, even imperfectly, He met me there. He didn't demand perfection, only honesty.

Faith, I learned, isn't about having every answer. It's not about being flawless or never doubting. It's about returning, again and again, to the One who made you. It's about letting Him shape your heart, one surrendered day at a time. Following God isn't about being perfect; it's about walking the path He sets before you, even when you can't see the end.

During this time, something unexpected happened. My brother asked me to officiate his wedding, and later, my family asked if I would baptize my niece. To do that, I needed to be ordained, so I sought an online ordination. At the time, I didn't see it as a step of faith. I saw it as a way to serve my family, to be there for them in moments that mattered. I wasn't thinking about ministry or calling; I was just trying to help. I didn't end up officiating my brother's marriage, or baptizing my niece, but something began to change inside me. I could feel the weight of what I was doing. I realized that I wasn't just serving my family. I was standing in moments where God was present.

Looking back, I see now that my ordination wasn't just a practical choice; it was a stepping-stone. It was one of those quiet moments where God used something ordinary to teach me something extraordinary. Through that experience, I began to understand that ministry isn't about titles or certificates. It's about obedience. It's about showing up when God gives you the chance to serve, even when you don't feel ready. That experience planted a seed in me that would later grow into a desire to learn, to write, and to share my faith more openly.

Now, when I think about my journey, I see how each chapter of my life has been a turning of the heart, from emptiness to searching, from searching to finding, and from finding to walking. God had been calling me all along, whispering through the quiet, through the pain, and through the people He placed in my life. And finally, I was learning to listen. I was learning that His voice doesn't always come through thunder or fire, but through gentle reminders that He has never left my side.

This chapter of my life was not about perfection, but direction. My heart was turning toward Him, and with every turn, I saw more of who He is and who I was meant to be. The walls that once separated me from peace were starting to crumble. What I did not realize yet was that the next step, the one that would change everything, was not about effort or achievement, but about something far greater. It was about grace.

Chapter 4 - Encounter With Grace

Before, when I was trying to get everything right all by myself, a single failure felt like the world was ending. I remember sitting there, head in my hands, feeling all of the joy leave me as I imagined how one mistake could undo everything I had worked for. Every small setback echoed in my mind for hours, sometimes days. Even when I managed to do something right, if it was not perfect, I convinced myself that it still was not enough. I measured my worth by how close I could get to flawless, and every time I fell short, I could almost hear a voice whisper that I would never be enough.

I tried to fix myself by working harder. I tried to be strong, stoic, and unshakable, but the truth was that I was tired. Every night felt like a performance where I was pretending to have it all together, only to collapse in exhaustion once I was alone. I wanted to be perfect, but perfection is a cruel master. It demands more than anyone can give, and it never stops asking.

Then one night, something changed. It was quiet in the room, the kind of quiet that almost hums, when I sat down to write a sermon. I had been working on messages for others, trying to help people find encouragement, but in that moment, I realized how much I needed encouragement myself. I was flipping through Scripture, searching for inspiration, when I stumbled across Romans 5:8. "But God demonstrates His own love for us in this: While we were still sinners, Christ died for us."

I remember reading it once, twice, and then again, each word settling deeper into my heart. It stopped me in my tracks. I had heard that verse before, but it had never felt personal until that moment. It was like God Himself was whispering it directly to me. Even with all my failures, all my brokenness, and all my stubborn pride, He had chosen to love me anyway. The perfect one chose to die for the imperfect one. The blameless chose to bear the blame of the broken. The one who never sinned chose to carry the weight of my sin so I would not have to.

I sat there for a long time, not sure whether to cry or smile. In that moment, I understood something that I had missed my whole life. Grace was not just an idea. It was a person. It was Jesus reaching out His hand to me and saying, "You do not have to fix yourself before you come to Me. I have already done what you could not."

It was the first time in my life that I truly felt peace. I was not proud or ashamed, not chasing or hiding. I was simply still, and loved.

Ephesians 2:8 says, "For it is by grace you have been saved, through faith, and this is not from yourselves; it is the gift of God." That verse came alive to me. I had spent so much of my life trying to earn love, approval, and forgiveness, but here was a truth that shattered that illusion completely. Grace is not earned. It is given. God does not weigh my good deeds against my bad ones. He does not look at my record and determine if I am worthy. He looks at His Son and says, "Because of Him, you are mine."

When I realized that, I felt a freedom I had never known before. The weight that I had carried for years, the shame, the fear of failing, and the need to prove myself began to lift. I told myself that if God could forgive my mistakes, then who was I to call them unforgivable? If God could look at me with compassion, then why could I not learn to do the same?

Grace changed not only how I saw God, but how I saw myself. It reminded me that I was not defined by what I had done, but by who He says I am. It also changed the way I looked at others. When I stopped holding myself to impossible standards, I found it easier to extend grace to the people around me. I could see their struggles without judgment, their failures without scorn, and their pain without comparison. I began to understand that grace is not a one-time event but a way of life.

The more I reflected on it, the more I saw grace woven through the story of my life. Every hardship I had faced, every failure I had endured, had prepared my heart for this revelation. Even the dark moments that I thought were wasted had been shaping me to understand what true love looks like. Grace was not just something I received. It was something God had been patiently teaching me to recognize all along.

I began to notice how grace had been showing up for years before I ever acknowledged it. When I was lost and hurting, grace came in the form of people who refused to give up on me. When I was too stubborn to pray, grace came as gentle conviction that stirred my heart. When I had no idea what to do with my life, grace came through small opportunities, little nudges toward something bigger that I could not yet see.

One of those nudges was my ministry. At first, I did not see it that way. When I began writing devotionals and sermons, it was simply something I felt drawn to do, something that gave me purpose. I wanted to help others understand God's love because I was finally beginning to see it for myself. But as I kept writing, I realized that my ministry, The Heart of What We Believe, was not born out of my own strength or wisdom. It was a direct product of grace.

God took a person who had once felt directionless, unworthy, and broken, and He used that same person to share His truth with others. That is what grace does. It redeems what seems useless and turns it into something beautiful. My ministry became a living reminder that grace is not just something we receive. It is something we live out. Every word I wrote, every message I shared, became a testimony to what God can do with a willing heart.

Sometimes people ask how I found the courage to start it, or where I found the confidence to preach and teach. The truth is, I did not have either on my own. What I had was gratitude. I was so thankful that God had chosen to love me in my brokenness that I wanted to share that love with anyone who would listen.

My ordination, at first, was not even a spiritual decision. I got ordained so I could officiate my brother's wedding and baptize my niece, two moments that were about family, not faith. But looking back, I can see how God used even that simple act as a stepping stone. What started as something small and ordinary became the foundation for a calling. He used it to open a door I did not even know was there.

That is how grace works. It takes what we see as coincidence and reveals purpose. It takes our small acts and turns them into holy moments. It shows us that God is always working, even in the things we least expect.

As time went on, I began to see grace not only in the big moments, but in the quiet ones. I saw it in the sunrise that reminded me of new beginnings, in the small answered prayers that seemed insignificant but spoke volumes about God's care. I saw it in forgiveness from people I had hurt, and in opportunities that came when I least deserved them. Grace was not limited to the pages of Scripture; it was alive in the everyday rhythm of my life.

There were days when I would be writing or praying, and I would suddenly feel an overwhelming peace wash over me. It was not dramatic or loud, just steady and sure, like a soft voice reminding me, "You are loved. You are enough." That is the quiet power of grace. It meets you where you are and reminds you that even in your smallest, most ordinary moments, God is near.

The more I grew in my understanding of grace, the more cohesive life became. Things that once seemed random or unfair began to make sense in light of God's purpose. Pain had meaning. Failure had lessons. And joy was no longer fleeting, but steady, rooted in something far deeper than circumstance. Grace taught me that peace does not come from everything going right, but from knowing that even when things go wrong, I am still loved.

I started seeing the beauty in imperfection. A project unfinished still had purpose. A conversation that went wrong still had grace in it. A plan that fell apart was sometimes an answer in disguise. Grace was not about getting everything right. It was about trusting that God's hand was in everything, even when I could not see it clearly.

When I finally accepted that, I began to live differently. I no longer chased perfection because I realized that the goal was not to be perfect but to be faithful. I began to write more, pray more, and trust more. I found joy in the process, even when the results were uncertain. I stopped fearing failure because I knew that God could use even my missteps for His glory.

Grace gave me freedom, not freedom to do whatever I wanted, but freedom to become who God always meant for me to be. It taught me that forgiveness is not the end of the story, but the beginning of transformation. Every day became a chance to start again, not because I had earned it, but because He had offered it.

Ephesians 2:8 remains one of my favorite verses because it reminds me of the simplicity of salvation. It is not complicated or earned. It is given freely to anyone who believes. Grace is the heartbeat of faith, the gentle rhythm that keeps us connected to God even when we stumble. It is what gives us the courage to keep walking, to keep growing, and to keep loving, not perfectly, but sincerely.

When I look at my life now, I see the fingerprints of grace everywhere. In the friendships that have endured, in the words that I have been given to share, and in the quiet moments when I feel peace that defies understanding. Grace has rewritten my story, turning what was once fractured into something whole. It has turned my failures into lessons and my weaknesses into testimonies.

And so, when I share my story, I share it with joy. Because the truth is, my story is not really about me. It is about the God who never stopped reaching for me. It is about the love that refused to let me stay broken. It is about grace that never gave up, even when I did.

Grace is not just the reason I am saved. It is the reason I keep going. It is what drives me to serve, to teach, and to live in a way that reflects the love that changed me. My ministry is not a monument to what I have done, but to what God continues to do through me. Every chapter I write, every message I share, is a reminder of that first night, the night when grace found me.

Even now, as I continue walking this path, I am constantly reminded that grace is still working. It has not stopped. It shapes my thoughts when I pray, my actions when I serve, and my words when I write. It teaches me to see the world with softer eyes, to listen more than I speak, and to love without expecting anything in return. It reminds me that I do not walk alone.

And as that grace continues to shape my life, I see that it is not a finish line, but a beginning. It is the start of renewal. The same grace that saved me is now inviting me to walk in newness of life. It whispers that the story is far from over, that repentance, growth, and joy are waiting on the next page.

That next page begins with understanding that when God's grace takes hold of your heart, it does not just forgive you. It changes you. It leads you away from who you were and draws you closer to who you were always meant to be. And that is where my journey continues, in repentance, in renewal, and in the joy of becoming a new creation in Christ.

Chapter 5 – Becoming New in Christ

When we are given new life in Christ, we are not the same person. The Holy Spirit comes down and takes up residence inside of us. We are renewed.

Grace does not only forgive us for our mistakes; it changes who we are at our core. It moves us to repentance, which is more than an apology. Repentance is a decision of the heart, a deep and honest turning toward God, and away from the things that once held us captive. When I realized what repentance truly was, it was not during a church service or after a sermon. It came quietly, painfully, and unexpectedly, in the middle of a struggle that had defined too much of my life.

For a long time, I did not want to admit that my addiction to online pornography was a problem. I told myself it was harmless, that it did not really hurt anyone, and that I could stop anytime I wanted. That was the lie that kept me chained. Each time

I gave in, I felt a momentary comfort followed by a crushing weight of guilt. I would promise myself it would be the last time, but before long, the cycle would begin again. Deep down, I knew I was a slave to it, but I did not want to face that truth.

When I first came before God with that struggle, I was not fully honest. I wanted to be forgiven, but I did not want to change. I prayed with half of my heart, asking God to take away the guilt while secretly holding onto the sin. For a while, nothing changed. The guilt would fade for a few days, then return, and I would fall again.

It was not until I truly understood grace that I began to understand repentance. I remember sitting alone one night, the room dark except for the dim light of a lamp beside me. I had just failed again, and the guilt felt unbearable. I sat there, staring at my hands, wondering why I could not be better. Why I could not just stop. Why I felt so powerless.

For the first time, I stopped pretending. I stopped trying to say the right words or sound spiritual. I just spoke. My prayer was raw and clumsy. I told God everything. I told Him I was ashamed. I told Him I was angry. I told Him I was tired of fighting a battle I could not win. I told Him I wanted to be different but did not know how. I told Him I did not want to live like this anymore. And then, for the first time, I sat in silence and waited.

What I felt in that silence was not condemnation or anger. It was peace. It was a still, quiet reminder that I was loved even in my failure. That moment changed me. It was not an instant transformation, but it was the beginning of a new kind of relationship with God. I realized that He did not want my perfection. He wanted my honesty.

The old me would have fought that battle alone. The old me would have believed that strength meant silence, and that asking for help was weakness. But when I accepted that God loved me, cared about me, and wanted what was best for me, I finally found the strength to stop. I was not acting for myself, or for another person's approval. I was acting out of love for God, wanting to honor Him in the way I lived. I no longer wanted to stand before Him in shame. I wanted to walk with Him in honesty and light.

When I let go of that addiction, it was as if I had cleaned out a long-neglected room. Years of dust and clutter, the kind you do not even realize has built up, were suddenly visible. It was painful to clear away, but freeing once I did. I threw out everything that reminded me of that darkness, every thought and habit that did not honor God. The relief was indescribable. I could finally breathe again.

That is what true repentance feels like. It is not just saying "I am sorry" and moving on. It is cleaning house, removing what keeps us from God, and inviting Him to fill those empty spaces with His presence. It is painful because it is real. It is humbling because it requires us to admit that we are powerless without Him. But it is also beautiful, because in that broken surrender, God begins to rebuild us.

Even now, there are moments when the temptation returns, when the old desires whisper in the back of my mind. But through prayer, I have learned to bring those moments straight to God. I do not hide them. I say, "Lord, this is still a part of me that needs Your strength." And He provides it. Every time I bring it to Him, it loses a little more of its power.

The verse that captures this truth for me is 2 Corinthians 5:17: "If anyone is in Christ, the new creation has come; the old has gone, the new is here." That verse is not a metaphor; it is a promise. When I turned to God, I became a new person. The old habits, the old lies, the old ways of finding comfort, they no longer define me. I am not who I once was.

When I think about that renewal, I also think of Psalm 51:10: "Create in me a clean heart, O God, and renew a right spirit within me." That prayer has become part of my daily rhythm. It reminds me that repentance is not a one-time event but a lifelong practice. Every day, God invites me to start fresh, to bring Him the parts of me that still need healing, and to trust that He can make them whole.

Repentance is not only about what we give up. It is about what we gain. When I let go of my sin, I gained peace. When I stopped hiding, I gained freedom. When I stopped fighting God's will, I gained strength. The Holy Spirit filled the empty space that sin had occupied, and I began to experience joy in ways I never had before.

One of the clearest signs of that renewal came when I began my ministry. I did not start it as an act of pride or because I thought I had all the answers. I started it because I wanted others to know that they were not alone. I had spent so much of my life feeling lost, ashamed, and disconnected from God, and I knew that others were struggling in the same ways. The ministry became a place for me to share what I had learned: that grace is real, forgiveness is possible, and renewal is for everyone.

The more I spoke about my journey, the more I realized how many people carried silent burdens. Some were battling addictions of their own. Others were trapped in guilt, convinced that they could never be forgiven. Some were simply tired of pretending. Every time someone reached out, I was reminded that God had taken my brokenness and turned it into something beautiful. My ministry was not about showcasing perfection; it was about showing how God works through imperfection.

That realization filled me with a deep and lasting joy. It was the kind of joy that does not depend on circumstances, but on knowing that my life, my story, and even my past were being used for something greater than myself. I started to see that the same grace that saved me was also working through me. My failures had become testimonies. My pain had become purpose.

Isaiah 1:18 says, "Though your sins are like scarlet, they shall be as white as snow." That verse captures exactly what I experienced. I had carried shame for so long that I forgot what it felt like to be clean. But when God washed me in His grace, He did not just wipe away the past. He gave me a new future.

I also learned that repentance is not just about sin. It is about mindset. There are days when I still have to repent of pride, selfishness, or fear. There are times when I catch myself worrying about things that I have already placed in God's hands. Repentance is not only for the big mistakes; it is for the small moments when we drift from God's presence. It is the act of realignment, of turning our eyes back toward Him again and again.

Every day, I pray for renewal. I ask God to help me be better than I was yesterday. If I fail to do something, I make it a point to do it twice as much the next time. If I speak harshly, I go back and apologize. If I fall short, I do not punish myself the way I once did. Instead, I thank God for showing me where I still need His help. That is what growth looks like.

For that opportunity to learn, I am joyful. I no longer have to sit in guilt and shame. Instead, I can learn, grow, and walk forward with confidence. When I started walking with God, life did not suddenly become easy, but it became peaceful. I no longer carry the same anxiety about who I am or what will happen next. My security is in Him.

I am grateful that God uses my past struggles, especially with mental health and addiction, to help others through their own. When I talk to someone who is hurting, I can say honestly, "I understand," because I have been there. I can tell them that healing is possible, not because I am strong, but because God is. That is the gift of repentance, it connects our stories to God's story.

We are all held back by something. Each of us has habits, fears, or sins that keep us from living fully in the life God has given us. Think about the first thing that comes to your mind. Maybe it is anger. Maybe it is envy. Maybe it is the need for control, or the fear of failure. Whatever it is, bring it to God. Pray and ask Him to help you overcome it. Then, when He begins that work, keep going. Do not stop at one victory. Repentance is a process, not an event. God will not only forgive you but will repurpose your struggles for His glory.

Every step we take toward Him is a step away from who we used to be. And that is what renewal really means. It is not about erasing the past; it is about transforming it. God takes our mistakes, our weaknesses, and our shame, and He uses them to create something new.

When I look back now, I do not see only failure. I see a trail of grace. Every place I stumbled became a place where God met me. Every mistake became an opportunity for growth. Every tear was a seed that God used to grow something new in me.

That is what 2 Corinthians 5:17 means to me. The old has gone. The new has come. I am not defined by who I was, but by who I am becoming in Christ. I am not the same person who once sought fulfillment in empty things. I am not the same person who hid from God out of shame. I am not the same person who thought repentance was a punishment. I am a new creation, reborn by grace and sustained by love.

Repentance is not the end of our story. It is the doorway into a new one. When we turn from our past, we do not simply walk away from something; we walk toward Someone. We begin to move in rhythm with the will of God, and our lives start to take on a new shape.

When I think about where I am now: serving in ministry, growing daily in faith, and helping others find their own path toward God, I cannot help but smile. It is not pride. It is gratitude. It is joy in knowing that even though I was once lost, I was found. Even though I was broken, I was made whole. Even though I was imperfect, I was loved perfectly.

That is what repentance and renewal are all about. They are not burdens, but blessings. They are not moments of loss, but moments of transformation. Every day that I wake up and choose to follow God is another day of renewal. Every prayer, every act of kindness, every moment of honesty brings me closer to the person He designed me to be.

And that is where the journey continues. Renewal is not a one-time gift. It is a daily grace. It is a heartbeat of faith, a rhythm of surrender, a constant invitation to walk closer with God.

The old has gone. The new has come. I am His, and I am free.

Chapter 6 – Learning to Walk in Faith

It may seem like I have everything together now, but I do not. I still face uncertainty every day. When I first renewed my faith, it felt incredible. I felt like I was on top of the world and that nothing could bring me down. There was such excitement in finally knowing God, in walking with Him, in feeling His presence close and real. Yet along with that joy came nervousness, even fear. It was like meeting someone new, except that Someone already knew everything about me. I had never had a strong relationship with Him before, and then suddenly I was giving my entire life to Him. That is a big step. It was humbling, thrilling, and frightening all at once.

Over time, I began praying more and reading scripture regularly. I asked questions about my own feelings, about my fears, about the things I did not understand. I learned that everything I felt was completely natural, and that what I needed most was not certainty but trust. I had to overcome my old habit of relying only

63

on myself and instead turn to God with everything that troubled me. It was hard to let go of control, but faith required me to release the reins. It was scary, but I had faith.

Even so, I doubted a lot. When I began choosing what direction my life would take, I started asking if it was what God had in mind for me. I prayed over every decision, sometimes so afraid of making a mistake that I felt frozen in place. I would sit in silence and ask God why He would fill my head with so many worries. I wanted clarity, and yet it often felt like the more I prayed, the less I understood. It was frustrating. Then one day I heard a message from Pastor Craig Groeschel, who said that God will not show us the entire path ahead. He shows us the next step. That changed everything for me. I realized that I had been demanding to see the whole map when all God wanted was for me to take one step forward in faith.

After that, I stopped trying to be three steps ahead. I began to focus on making the next right step instead of controlling the whole journey. It lifted a weight off of me, though sometimes I still struggle with it. I am learning patience. I am learning that God does not need me to know the plan. He simply asks me to trust that He is in control. Faith, I realized, does not replace fear or worry. It gives us a place to put it. When I feel anxious or uncertain now, I take those feelings to God instead of letting them bury me. I began to see Him in small things, in little reminders that He was near. If God can remember a bird in flight or the flower in the field, then surely He can remember me when I need guidance.

With this newfound faith, I began to see everything differently. I stopped worrying about whether things would turn out exactly the way I imagined. Instead, I focused on doing my best in each situation, trusting that God would handle the rest. This was especially important in my ministry work. When I would sit down to write, I would worry that I would say something wrong or that I would not say what someone needed to hear. I used to stare at the page for hours, afraid that my words might fail someone. But once I remembered that the words are not mine alone, I could breathe again. I would write what God placed on my heart and trust Him to use it in the way He saw fit.

I also began to release the need to control others. Before, I wanted everything and everyone around me to operate by my standards. I thought that if I could get people to act the way I wanted, then my life would finally make sense. But that was not faith, that was fear disguised as control. Faith taught me that I cannot dictate every outcome. I can only control my own actions, my own heart, and my own response to what happens. That change brought peace. When I stopped fighting to make everything go my way, I discovered that life was far more joyful. I was no longer trying to force God's plan into my image. I was learning to fit myself into His.

Faith also taught me that trying to do my best is enough. I still fall short sometimes. I still make mistakes. But through faith, I have learned that those mistakes are not the end of the story. God uses them to teach me, to shape me, to make me better. As long as I continue to trust in Him, He will keep molding me into who I am meant to be. That has been one of the most freeing realizations of my entire life.

My faith eventually led me to begin my ministry. At first, I was hesitant. I did not feel qualified. I wondered how someone like me, with my past mistakes and my ongoing struggles, could speak about the things of God. Yet there was this persistent feeling, a quiet but firm calling. It felt as though God was saying, "I have prepared you for this." I wrestled with it for weeks, unsure if it was truly Him or just my own thoughts. But the calling only grew stronger. Finally, I decided to take the step, and I have never been happier.

My ministry began as an act of obedience, a simple "yes" to God. Since then, I have found it to be one of the greatest blessings of my life. Every time I write, speak, or pray over someone, I take faith with me. I have faith in God, and faith that He will speak through me. There are times when I still doubt myself, when I think I do not have the right words or that I will not say something the way I should. But in those moments, I remember the promise that the Holy Spirit will give me the words when I need them. I am not speaking on my own. I am simply a vessel for what God is trying to say.

One of the most profound experiences I ever had happened while I was traveling in India. During one of the ministry events there, I was asked to pray for an injured woman. She had been suffering from pain for quite some time, and I was nervous. I did not know what to say or how to pray in that moment. But I remembered what I had learned. Faith does not demand understanding. It asks for trust. So I laid my hand gently on her shoulder and began to pray. I asked God to bring her peace, to ease her pain, and to let His will be done in her life. I did not use any special words. I just prayed from the heart, sincerely and quietly. When we finished, she thanked me and walked away slowly. I did not think much of it at the time.

About a week later, I was told that the woman had been healed. The pain that had plagued her for so long was completely gone. I sat there, speechless. I had never felt such awe. It was not about me or my words. It was about what God had done through faith. I had prayed believing that He could act, but seeing that prayer answered so directly humbled me in a way I will never forget. That moment solidified something in me that I had only known in theory before. Faith is not about our strength. It is about our surrender. It is about believing that God will move even when we cannot see how.

Since that time, I have prayed over many people. I have seen miracles, both large and small. I have seen hearts softened, lives restored, and hope rekindled. Every time, I am reminded that faith is alive and active. It is not a theory or an emotion. It is a living relationship with the God who loves us beyond measure. Each act of faith, no matter how small, opens the door a little wider for His presence to enter.

Walking in faith has not made life easier, but it has made it richer. When I face challenges now, I do not face them alone. I bring them to God, and even when the answer is not immediate, I find peace in knowing that He hears me. Sometimes His answer is yes. Sometimes it is no. Sometimes it is "wait." And I am learning that all three are acts of love. Waiting has become one of the hardest but most transformative parts of my walk with God. It is in the waiting that my trust deepens and my heart learns patience.

Faith has also reshaped the way I see success. I used to measure everything by results. Now I measure it by obedience. If I have done what God asked me to do, then I have succeeded, no matter what the outcome looks like. That perspective has brought peace to my heart and has removed so much of the pressure I used to put on myself. I no longer need to have all the answers. I only need to be faithful with what I am given.

There are days when fear still creeps in. There are moments when I still feel inadequate. But faith does not mean those feelings disappear. It means that I know what to do with them. When the doubts come, I take them to prayer. When anxiety builds, I remind myself that God has never failed me. When I feel unworthy, I remember that He calls me His own. Each time, I come back to the same truth that has carried me since the beginning: faith is confidence in what we hope for and assurance in what we do not yet see.

The more I walk in faith, the more I notice God's fingerprints everywhere. In conversations that come at the perfect time, in opportunities that align too perfectly to be coincidence, in the quiet moments when I feel peace settle over me for no apparent reason. It is as though He is always whispering, "I am here." Faith trains our eyes to see what was there all along.

My ministry continues to grow because of that faith. Each message I write, each devotional I prepare, feels like an offering to God. It is not about perfection or popularity. It is about obedience and love. I do not always know who will read the words or how they will be received, but I trust that God will send them to the right person. Sometimes someone reaches out to tell me that something I wrote gave them peace or helped them through a hard time. Those moments are reminders that even the smallest act of faith can ripple farther than we ever imagine.

Learning to walk in faith has been a lifelong lesson. I am still learning every day. It is not a single moment of arrival but an ongoing journey of trust. Faith does not promise that the road will be easy, but it promises that the road will never be walked alone. God walks with us through every valley and over every mountain. His presence is the light that guides us when we cannot see the way ahead.

If you are wondering how to begin, start small. Take one step toward God today. Ask Him what He wants you to trust Him with. Maybe it is a relationship, a dream, a fear, or a decision you have been putting off. Whatever it is, offer it to Him in prayer. Let faith lead you even if the path is uncertain. Remember that every great journey begins with one step, and God will meet you wherever you are.

Faith is a daily action, not a one-time choice. It is walking with love and compassion in our hearts and striving to be the best we can be, even when we do not understand. It is choosing to see God in every circumstance and trusting that His plan is always for our good. We do not have to know where the road leads, because we know the One who leads us. When we walk with Him, we may not always understand the steps, but we can be certain of this: we will never walk alone.

Chapter 7 – Faith that Endures

It may seem like I have all my stuff together now, but I don't. I still face uncertainty every day. When I first renewed my faith, it felt incredible. I felt like I was on top of the world, as if nothing could bring me down. For the first time, I knew God, and I was excited to walk with Him. But at the same time, I was nervous. It was like meeting someone new and trying to understand who they are. I hadn't ever had a strong relationship with God before, and suddenly, I was giving my whole life to Him. That's a big commitment. It's exciting, but also scary.

Over time, I began praying more, reading Scripture, and asking questions about my own feelings. I started to learn that what I was feeling was completely natural. Most of the time, it came down to trust. I had to learn to trust God's process for me, even when I didn't understand it. That was hard. I had spent most of my life relying on myself, on what I could control. Turning that over to God felt uncomfortable at first. I wasn't used to handing over the steering wheel. But I did, one situation at a time, and each time I did, I found a little more peace.

I doubted a lot. I still do sometimes. When I began deciding what to do with my life, I prayed over everything. I wanted to make sure that every move I made was in line with what God wanted for me. I would pray and then wait, wondering if what I was hearing or feeling was truly from Him. I would ask God to give me clarity, but sometimes things would only get muddier. There were nights when I asked Him why He would put so many worries in my mind, or why He would let me sit in confusion. It was frustrating, but I kept praying anyway. I didn't know it then, but I was learning how to walk by faith and not by sight.

I remember listening to a sermon one day, where I heard something that changed my perspective. The pastor said that God doesn't show us the entire path ahead, only where to step next. I realized then that faith wasn't about knowing everything that was coming; it was about trusting God one step at a time. I didn't need to see the full plan. I just needed to see the next right step and take it faithfully. That realization changed me. I stopped trying to live three steps ahead and started focusing on what I could do today.

It didn't make things easy. In fact, sometimes it made things harder. Letting go of control isn't simple. But I started to notice that when I stopped worrying about what was ahead, I had more peace about what was right in front of me. When things went wrong, I didn't panic as much. I knew that even when I couldn't see what was happening, God could. That's what faith is: walking forward in the dark, knowing that the hand guiding you will never let go.

Faith also changed how I approached the small, ordinary things in my life. Before, I used to think faith was only about the big moments: crises, decisions, or major life changes. But I began to understand that faith lives in the daily moments, too. It's in waking up early to pray when you're tired. It's in choosing patience when you're frustrated. It's in showing kindness when no one's watching. Faith is obedience in the small things, because those small things build who we are.

There are days when I don't want to write devotionals or record my sermons. I'd rather rest, watch a movie, or do anything else. But I've learned that faith is not about waiting until I feel inspired; it's about showing up for God even when I don't. Discipline is an act of worship. When I push through the feeling of not wanting to, I always feel a deep joy afterward. It's as though God smiles when we choose obedience over comfort.

I've also realized that faith isn't about results, it's about consistency. I've had times where I poured my heart into a message, then saw almost no engagement. I would check the numbers and feel discouraged. I would wonder if I was wasting my time, or if anyone cared about what I said. But then, quietly, someone would send me a message telling me how that devotional spoke to them, or how something I wrote made them stop and think. That's when I remember: I don't do this for numbers or applause. I do it for the one who needs to hear it, and ultimately, for the One who sent me to share it.

Sometimes I think about that unknown person: the one who finds my post by accident late at night, when they're at their lowest, and they read a line that gives them hope. I may never know who they are, but God does. And if my obedience plants even one seed in their heart, that's enough. The numbers don't tell the story; God does. My ministry isn't about recognition, it's about reflection. I want my work to reflect the God who changed me.

Faith also started to appear in how I approached my daily work. I began praying on my drive, not about anything in particular, but whatever came to mind. Sometimes I would thank God for the sunrise. Sometimes I would ask Him to help me be kind, or to bless someone else's day. It became a habit, one that turned my ordinary commute into time spent with my Creator. When I got to work, I would remind myself to be a light, even in small ways. A kind word, a smile, or just listening to someone could change their whole day.

I'm not naturally cheerful all the time. But I've learned that even a small act of love, even when I'm tired, can make a big difference. Faith teaches us to look beyond ourselves, to care even when it's inconvenient. I've learned to ask myself each day: "How can I be a blessing to someone today?" That one question changes everything.

There have been moments when I've felt like God was silent. When prayers seemed unanswered, and I felt like I was speaking into the air. In those moments, I've reminded myself that silence isn't absence. Sometimes, God is working quietly in ways I can't see yet. Other times, He's teaching me patience. The hardest part of faith is waiting, but it's also the part where growth happens.

Through all of this, I've come to see that faith is not a feeling; it's a decision. It's not something that depends on how spiritual we feel on any given day. It's a steady trust that remains even when the emotions fade. I think about Galatians 6:9 often: "Let us not become weary in doing good, for at the proper time we will reap a harvest if we do not give up." That verse reminds me that what I'm doing now matters, even if I can't see the results yet. Perseverance is one of the purest forms of faith.

There's also a kind of faith that comes from enduring the ordinary. We're quick to thank God in the miracles and lean on Him in the crises, but faith also means trusting Him in the uneventful, repetitive days. The truth is, most of life is made up of small, quiet moments. And if we can keep our faith alive there, then our relationship with God becomes unshakable.

Faith also calls me to fight against my own comfort. There are Sundays when I don't want to get up for church. The bed feels warm, my body is tired, and the idea of getting dressed and going out feels like too much. But every time I go, I'm reminded of why I do it. God shows up when we show up. The same goes for prayer, writing, and worship. Every time I choose to get up instead of giving in, my faith grows stronger.

Faith isn't passive; it's active. It's something we live. When I feel myself slipping into frustration or anger, I try to stop, breathe, and remember who I am in Christ. I'm not perfect, but I am forgiven. I'm not always patient, but I'm learning. I'm not always joyful, but I am loved. That's what faith tells us: that even when we fall short, God's hand is still on our shoulder, guiding us forward.

I've learned that the best way to endure in faith is to remember where it started. Every time I think back to when I first discovered grace, it reminds me why I do what I do. I'm not just living for myself anymore. I'm living for the One who saved me. That truth gives me strength when I want to quit, and peace when I don't understand.

Faith is also about hope. Even when the future feels uncertain, I trust that God is working. Philippians 1:6 reminds me that the good work God started in me will not stop until it is complete. That verse gives me comfort. It means that every trial, every lesson, every success and failure is part of His plan to make me more like Him.

Over time, I've realized that endurance in faith is a form of love. God has never stopped being faithful to me, so why should I stop being faithful to Him? When I stay steady through doubt, fear, and fatigue, I am showing my love for the One who never left me.

Through my ministry, my daily habits, and even my smallest choices, I've learned that faith is something that matures quietly. It doesn't need to shout. It just needs to keep showing up. That's the beauty of walking with God: you don't always feel the change happening, but one day, you look back and realize how far He's brought you.

Even when things seem slow, I know God is moving. His plan unfolds in ways we can't predict, and sometimes that plan includes seasons of silence or stillness. Faith tells me that those moments aren't wasted, they're preparation. God is always shaping something new inside us, even when we can't see it.

Faith that endures is not loud or dramatic. It's steady. It's the prayer whispered in the dark. It's the devotion written after a long day. It's the willingness to show love even when no one notices. It's finding God in the quiet spaces of life and trusting that He's still at work.

Now, when I look at my life, I see faith everywhere. In the early morning prayers, in the ministry that continues to grow, in the people whose lives I've touched without even knowing it. Each of these things is a reminder that faith doesn't have to be perfect to be powerful. It just has to be real.

And that's what I hope others see through my story: not a perfect Christian, but a persistent one. Someone who keeps walking, even when the road is unclear. Someone who keeps believing, even when the world is quiet. Someone who trusts, even when they don't understand. That's what faith is: not the absence of doubt, but the courage to keep walking anyway.

I've learned that faith and grace go hand in hand. Faith helps us endure the journey, and grace carries us through it. Every day I live, I see new ways that God's grace meets me where I am. It's in the forgiveness I didn't deserve, the peace I didn't earn, and the strength I didn't know I had.

When we have faith that endures, grace becomes part of our every day. It shapes the way we speak, act, and love. And it prepares us for what's next. For me, what's next is learning to live in that grace; to see it in the simple moments, to breathe it in with gratitude, and to share it freely with others.

Because faith that endures doesn't just survive, it grows. And when it grows, it leads us into something even deeper. It leads us into a life of everyday grace.

Chapter 8 – Grace for the Everyday

I was driving the other day, and I got cut off in traffic. Does that sound familiar? How did you react? Me personally, I got pretty irked. I mean, come on, I was right there! So, I rolled my eyes, said a few curse words, and pouted for a little bit. Then, I prayed. I prayed for myself, so I wouldn't be as angry, and I prayed for the other driver. It sounds kind of counterintuitive, but I couldn't help but feel guilty afterward.

When I cursed at them, I was coming from a place of anger. The first thing I wanted to do was to ask God to take that anger away and to support me. The second thing I wanted to do was to ask God to do what I couldn't and assist that other driver to have a better day. While our emotions are fleeting, we often find ourselves with outbursts, whether they be joy, sorrow, or anger. I had no way of knowing what that driver was going through, and I also know that God gives us new beauty to witness every day of our lives. Why should I let something small ruin the beauty and wonder that God put before me today? Grace toward others is just as important as grace in a crisis.

When I first started learning all of this, I thought that grace was only for the big stuff, like sin, forgiveness, and redemption; those life-changing moments. I believed grace was given to us so that we could be worthy in God's eyes, but that it only applied to spiritual milestones. But no, that's not right. Grace doesn't only show up in the life-altering moments. It's also present in the small, quiet spaces where we least expect it.

Grace is also found when someone insults us and we don't fire back with a snappy quip. It's found when we forgive someone for cutting us off in traffic, or when we admit we're wrong, even when it bruises our pride. All of these things show grace being lived out in things that we already should be doing every day. They're small acts of mercy that reflect God's mercy toward us.

Lamentations 3:22–23 says, "Because of the Lord's great love we are not consumed, for his compassions never fail. They are new every morning; great is your faithfulness." That verse reminds me that every single day, God gives us a fresh supply of grace. It's not like an allowance that runs out when we've made too many mistakes. God's mercy doesn't have a limit. He gives us all the grace we need to live through each and every day, knowing full well that we'll stumble and fall. Every sunrise is proof of His patience and love, a sign that yesterday's failures do not define today's walk.

That verse also means something else. It means that God's love isn't reactive, it's proactive. He doesn't just wait for us to fail and then hand out mercy like a bandage. His grace is already there when we wake up, ready to meet us before the day even begins. He knows what mistakes we'll make, what moments will test us, and what temptations we'll face. And still, He gives us compassion before we even ask. That kind of love is humbling.

I woke up a few days ago just irritated at the world. I had a long list of things to do, and honestly, I didn't want to get out of bed. I felt overwhelmed before the day even started. My alarm went off, and I reached for my phone with a heavy sigh. When I went to turn it off, I noticed the Bible app notification for the verse of the day. I figured it couldn't hurt to read it. The verse was about peace and endurance, and it spoke to exactly what I was feeling. I took a deep breath, prayed to God to help me through the day, and asked Him to let my actions glorify Him. That small moment of grace changed my entire mood. By the time I got out of bed, I was lighter. I wasn't magically joyful, but I was calm, centered, and ready to face what was ahead.

Grace has a way of meeting us right where we are, even in the smallest, most mundane moments. Sometimes we think God's presence is only felt in miracles or worship services, but His grace lives in the ordinary. It's in the morning sunlight coming through your blinds. It's in the smile of a stranger. It's in the quiet peace that comes when you finally stop trying to control everything and let God handle it.

In my daily life, I get frustrated, especially at work. I see a lot of people come and go, and I have to be kind to all of them. Some days, I just don't want to. Maybe I didn't sleep well, or something's been bothering me, and I'm tired of pretending everything's fine. But even on those days, when someone comes to my desk asking for help, I remind myself that they don't deserve to be on the receiving end of my frustration. So I smile, put my problems aside, and help them. It's not always easy, but that small act of kindness gives me a little grace in return. Sometimes, someone else's kindness comes back to me when I least expect it, and it shifts my entire outlook. That's the beauty of grace: it multiplies when we give it away.

It's not always easy to be graceful, but I've come to realize that grace is God's love acting through me. Every time I choose patience over anger, or kindness over irritation, I'm giving someone a small piece of the love that God gives me every day. I make a conscious decision, when I'm angry, to be kind. That's giving grace that I don't have to, but I want to, because I want to reflect the love of Christ. The same grace that I show to others, God shows to me when I mess things up.

If I asked for God's grace but refused to show grace to others, I'd be like the servant in the parable who was forgiven a great debt but couldn't forgive his fellow servant for a much smaller one. It's easy to forget that the grace we receive comes with responsibility. We aren't meant to hoard it; we're meant to share it.

Still, I'm far from perfect. I have moments when I forget to be kind and gracious. I get overwhelmed, snap at someone, and say something harsh that they don't deserve. It's a terrible feeling. I remember one time when I said something unkind to a coworker after he made a few comments about me being late to work. It had only been a few minutes here and there, but it bothered me, and instead of talking about it calmly, I snapped. I reminded him that he had been thirty minutes late the week before for an appointment with his child. I knew it wasn't fair of me to say that.

Afterward, I felt awful. The guilt sat heavy in my chest. I couldn't shake it. I went to my boss, who's also a mentor to me, and told him what happened. I said that the next time I saw that coworker, I would apologize. When I did, my coworker brushed it off and said it was fine, but I knew it wasn't fine with me. The guilt had eaten away at me because I knew I was wrong, and I couldn't make peace with myself until I made peace with him.

That moment taught me something important about grace. I realized that the conviction I felt wasn't meant to shame me; it was meant to lead me back to humility. God's grace didn't condemn me for that outburst; it invited me to make things right. When I asked forgiveness from God and from my coworker, I felt a weight lift off my shoulders. Grace humbled me, and that humility brought healing.

Through my ministry, my work, and my relationships, I try to show grace wherever I can. When I apologized to that coworker, it opened a door for better understanding between us. It gave me an opportunity to explain how I had been feeling, and it encouraged him to be more mindful too. What could have stayed as quiet resentment became a moment of connection and growth. That's what grace does: it repairs what pride would rather leave broken.

I still look for places where I can exercise grace with others every single day, because God does the same for me. He doesn't just give grace every day; He delights in it. God loves to give grace. He loves to forgive, to comfort, and to guide us. He delights in taking care of us and loving us even when we are at our worst.

When I stop to think about it, that's one of the most beautiful parts of the Christian life. God never gives grace reluctantly. He gives it with joy. He looks at us, fully aware of our flaws and failures, and still says, "You are mine. I will not give up on you." When we receive that kind of love, it changes us. It softens us. It helps us extend that same love to others, even when they don't deserve it.

Everyday grace is not about perfection; it's about presence. It's about being aware of how God moves through your day, in the quiet moments and in the chaos. It's in the patience you show when you are in line at the grocery store and the cashier is taking longer than usual. It's in the forgiveness you offer when a friend says something hurtful. It's in the calmness you choose when you're stuck in traffic, remembering that there's no sense in letting one small moment steal your peace.

Grace also teaches me to slow down. So often, I rush through my days, trying to check everything off my list. I get frustrated when things don't move as fast as I want them to. But grace whispers, "Take a breath." It reminds me that every moment is a chance to grow, to learn, to be patient, to love better. God doesn't rush us to perfection; He walks with us through every step.

Some of the most powerful moments of grace I've experienced have come when I least deserved them. There have been times when I've failed to live up to my calling, when I've been lazy, irritable, or distracted. And yet, in those moments, God meets me with patience. He doesn't scold me for falling short. Instead, He gently reminds me that His grace is still there, waiting for me to pick up where I left off.

Grace also changes the way I see others. Before, I used to measure people by how they treated me. If someone was rude, I'd write them off. But now, I try to see them the way God sees them: as people in need of grace, just like me. When someone is short with me, I ask myself what they might be going through. Maybe they're struggling with something I don't know about. Maybe they're having a hard day. Maybe they just need someone to show them a little compassion. That perspective changes everything.

There's something powerful about realizing that grace is not just a concept; it's a lifestyle. It's how we live out God's love in a world that desperately needs it. When I show grace to someone, even in a small way, I'm showing them a glimpse of God's character. That's a humbling thought.

Grace doesn't just forgive us, it transforms us. It reshapes the way we see the world, the way we treat others, and the way we treat ourselves. It's easy to show grace to strangers sometimes, but much harder to show it to ourselves. Yet, every time we fail, God invites us to stand back up and try again. That's what it means when Scripture says His mercies are new every morning. Every sunrise is a reminder that we have another chance to live with love, patience, and gratitude.

I try to start each morning now with that in mind. Before I reach for my phone or start making plans for the day, I take a moment to thank God for another chance to live in His grace. I ask Him to guide my thoughts, my words, and my actions. And I ask Him to help me see others through His eyes. When I do that, the day feels lighter, and even the small annoyances seem more manageable.

Grace isn't about pretending everything is fine or forcing a smile. It's about knowing that God's presence is enough to sustain us through whatever comes. It's about letting His love overflow into the lives of those around us. It's about remembering that every act of kindness, every moment of patience, and every word of encouragement is a reflection of His heart.

I don't always get it right. None of us do. But every day, I get another chance to try again. That's what grace means to me: it's the daily renewal of hope that says, "You are not finished yet. God is still at work in you."

When I think about all the ways God has shown me mercy, I can't help but want to show it to others. Through my ministry, through my words, and through my actions, I want people to see the same grace that saved me. Because when we live with grace, we invite others to experience the God who gives it freely.

God's grace doesn't just save us, it sustains us. It carries us through each moment, no matter how small. Whether it's forgiving a driver on the road, apologizing to a coworker, or simply choosing patience, every act of grace draws us closer to Him. And as we walk in that grace, we begin to see that it's not just something to receive, but something to live.

Everyday grace teaches us to see holiness in the ordinary. It reminds us that God is not distant; He's right here, in the middle of our daily lives, turning frustration into peace and impatience into love. His mercies are truly new every morning, and His faithfulness never fails.

The more I live, the more I see that grace is not just what saves us, it's what keeps us. It's what makes each day worth living. And as I continue to walk with God, I see that grace is not the end of the story, it's the beginning of a life lived fully for Him.

And that life, lived in His grace, leads to something even greater: the call to take that grace and put it into action.

Chapter 9 – Living Out Love

I used to have my own idea of what love is. I used to watch an emotional movie or read a book filled with perfect words and perfect endings, and I thought that was what real love looked like. I believed that love meant finding someone who completed you, who made you feel good, and who never left. It was an idea built on feelings rather than faith. I chased after it, convinced that I could find the version of love that would fix the emptiness I felt inside. It definitely hurt more than one relationship I was in, because that is not the true form of love that we should know first.

When I came to understand God's love for me, everything changed. I learned that there are different types of love in the Greek language, and one of them, called agape, completely reshaped how I viewed it. Agape means selfless, sacrificial, unconditional love. It is the kind of love that gives without expecting anything in return. That is the love that God feels for us, and it opened my eyes to what love could be.

Not only am I supposed to love people I like, but I am also supposed to love people I do not like. That was something difficult for me to understand. If I do not like someone, why should I love them? Why should I be kind to people who have hurt me, insulted me, or ignored me? Why should I forgive people who have never said they were sorry?

It was around this time that I came across a verse in Genesis that answered the question perfectly. It says that we are all created in the image of God. That truth alone shifted my perspective. Every person I meet, whether I get along with them or not, carries the image of the Creator. Every face, every voice, every person who walks past me bears a piece of the One who made us all. If for no other reason than that, I should choose to love people, because loving them is a form of loving God.

That realization gave me peace, but it also challenged me deeply. It is easy to love people who love us back. It is easy to care for those who are kind and respectful. But love takes on a whole new meaning when it is given to those who have not earned it. That is what agape looks like in practice. It is not about feelings or rewards, but about reflection, the reflection of God's heart through our own.

It also helped me to know that God loved me first, because that love allowed me to love others without needing validation. I did not have to prove my worth or earn affection anymore. I wanted people to feel loved in the same way that I had been loved by God. The more I experienced His grace, the more I wanted to extend that same grace to others.

Forgiveness was one of the hardest ways for me to show love. I have been known to hold grudges. I used to believe that holding on to my anger gave me control, that somehow refusing to forgive would protect me from being hurt again. But when I learned about God's love, I realized that forgiveness was not a sign of weakness. It was an act of strength.

Forgiveness does not mean forgetting what happened. I still remember the people who bullied me in school, the words that cut deep, and the relationships that ended painfully. I remember the betrayal, the silence, and the moments I felt abandoned. But I do not hold that anger anymore. I have learned to give that pain to

God and ask Him to show me how to love even those who wounded me.

That does not mean that everyone I forgive gets to be a part of my life again. Boundaries are still important. There are people I have forgiven who I will never allow close again, not out of bitterness, but out of wisdom. Forgiveness is not about erasing the past, but about releasing the power it has over your heart. We do not forgive for the sake of the other person alone. We forgive for our own healing and for God's glory.

True love is not a feeling that comes and goes. It is a choice we make every single day. It is an action we take when we offer grace, patience, or kindness even when it is difficult. When we forgive someone, we are not saying what they did was right. We are saying that God's mercy is bigger than the hurt they caused.

Over time, I began to see how small acts of love could make a big difference. I try to show love through simple gestures, like buying someone a coffee, paying for a meal, giving my time to someone who needs to talk, or even just sending a message to check in on someone who has been quiet. These things are not elaborate or impressive, but they carry meaning. Sometimes, the smallest act of love can speak louder than the most eloquent speech.

One moment that stands out to me was when a friend called late at night. They were struggling, and all they needed was someone to listen. I did not have any words of wisdom or solutions to give, but I stayed on the phone while they cried. I just listened. Sometimes love is as simple as being present. That call lasted over an hour, and at the end of it, they said, "Thank you for being here." That was it. I hung up and realized that love does not always need grand gestures. It needs sincerity.

My ministry has helped me see love from countless new angles. When I first began speaking about love, I thought I understood it fairly well. But the more I researched, prayed, and preached, the more I realized that love is far more expansive than I could have imagined. When I prepared a sermon about love, I dove into Scripture, exploring not just the command to love but the way Jesus demonstrated it. He did not just preach love. He lived it.

Then, I began preaching that same message to others, and I got to see what love looks like in real time. One of the most powerful moments for me came when I spoke to a congregation in India. I remember logging on for the service and being amazed by how devoted they were. The way they praised and worshiped God, the way they held onto every word, it was humbling. I could feel their love for the Lord radiating through the screen. They were not just listening to me. They were worshiping with me. I could sense their joy, their humility, and their genuine affection for God and for one another. That was agape love in motion.

It taught me that love is not limited by distance, culture, or language. Love speaks a universal language that everyone can understand. That moment renewed my faith in what I was doing. It reminded me that love can travel farther than we ever will, and that when we act in love, God uses it in ways we may never see.

God's love for me has changed how I speak, how I act, and how I think. It has softened my tone when I want to be sharp. It has taught me to pause before reacting. It has made me more compassionate toward others and more patient with myself. I have learned that love requires humility, because without humility, love becomes prideful. God's love has taught me to look for peace rather than victory, and to choose understanding over being right.

It has also changed how I view myself. There are still days when I look in the mirror and feel disappointment. I see the flaws, the scars, and the memories of mistakes I wish I could erase. But then I remember that I am fearfully and wonderfully made. God does not make mistakes. He created me intentionally, and I fit His plan exactly as He designed. I am not perfect, but I am perfectly His.

When I began to see myself through that lens, I realized something important. If I can see myself with love and grace, I can see others that way too. The same grace I receive every morning is the grace I am called to give to others. Every person I meet is another opportunity to live out God's love.

Love is the thread that ties together everything else I have learned in my walk with Christ. It connects grace, repentance, forgiveness, and joy into a single, beautiful tapestry. Without love, grace is empty. Without love, repentance is cold. Without love, forgiveness feels forced. Love gives meaning to them all.

I have seen this truth in my ministry time and time again. There have been moments when someone has written to me after a devotional, saying that it helped them feel closer to God. Some have said it gave them peace in a moment of chaos. Others have said it helped them forgive someone they thought they never could. Those words remind me that love, when shared through the Gospel, multiplies endlessly. Every person who receives it becomes a vessel to carry it further.

Love is not just about comfort. It is also about accountability. Real love does not ignore sin or wrongdoing. It guides us back to truth. Jesus showed this when He corrected His disciples, when He forgave those who crucified Him, and when He called out hypocrisy not out of hate but out of love for their souls. That kind of love requires courage. It is not always easy, but it is always worth it.

Every time I write a devotional or speak in front of others, I pray that my words are filled with love. Not the sentimental kind that fades, but the enduring kind that reflects the heart of God. Love that encourages, uplifts, and challenges people to grow closer to Him. Love that reminds people that they are seen, valued, and cherished beyond measure.

I have also learned that love is not always loud. Sometimes it is quiet. It shows up in patience, in listening, in simply showing up for someone without needing recognition. Love is in the act of sitting beside someone who is grieving, offering comfort without words. It is in celebrating others' victories without jealousy. It is in the silent prayers we say for someone who may never know we prayed for them.

This kind of love takes practice. It requires daily effort and constant reminders. Some days, I fail. I get impatient, I speak harshly, I forget to love as I should. But the beauty of God's love is that it allows me to start over every time. His love never runs out. It invites me to learn again and again what it means to love like Him.

The world often tells us that love is a transaction. You give some to get some back. But God's love breaks that pattern completely. He loved us before we ever loved Him. He loved us knowing we would fail, betray, and deny Him. He loved us so deeply that He sent His Son to die for us. That is the love we are called to reflect. Not conditional or self-serving, but eternal.

It is not always easy to love people the way God does. Some people make it difficult. There will always be those who test our patience, who hurt us, or who seem ungrateful for what we offer. But every time we choose to love anyway, we grow closer to God. Love becomes an act of worship.

When I think about 1 John 4:19, "We love because He first loved us," I am reminded that everything starts with Him. Every ounce of compassion, every act of service, every word of forgiveness comes from knowing that He loved us first. That verse takes the pressure off. I do not have to manufacture love from my own strength. I just have to pass along the love I have already received.

Now, I try to live with that in mind every day. Whether I am at work, talking to a stranger, spending time with family, or writing a message for my ministry, I ask myself how I can show love in that moment. Sometimes it means speaking truth gently. Sometimes it means being quiet and listening. Sometimes it means giving something up for the sake of another.

Love is not a one-time choice. It is a daily decision to walk in grace, to forgive quickly, to be patient, and to remember that every person I encounter is loved by God just as much as I am.

I want to invite you, as you read this, to think about one person you can show love to this week. It does not have to be dramatic. It could be a simple message, a smile, a conversation you have been avoiding, or even a quiet prayer for someone who is struggling. Love does not always need to be seen to be powerful. Sometimes the smallest seed of kindness can grow into something eternal.

Because in the end, love is what ties everything together. It is the evidence of God's Spirit at work in us. It is what transforms brokenness into healing and doubt into peace. It is what brings light into dark places and hope into weary hearts.

Love is the reflection of the God who made us, saved us, and walks with us still. It is not the end of the story. It is the heartbeat of every chapter that comes after.

And as we learn to live out that love, we begin to understand something even deeper. Love is not only what God gives. It is who He is.

Chapter 10 – Purpose and Calling

I have asked a lot, especially these last couple of years as I have transitioned through life, "What am I meant to do?" It sounds like such a simple question on the surface, but it is one that has kept me awake at night, staring at the ceiling and wondering what my next step was supposed to be. I have spent countless hours thinking about my future, my goals, and my purpose. For a long time, I chased what I wanted to do rather than what God wanted me to do. I found things that brought me a short sense of happiness, and for a time, I thought that was enough. But the joy never lasted.

I would pour myself into hobbies or distractions, thinking that they would give me meaning. Sometimes they worked for a little while, but deep down, I always knew that something was missing. There was an ache that nothing else could fill, no matter how hard I tried. It was not until I started this ministry that I began to understand what purpose really means.

When I first began, my life changed drastically. Suddenly, I had so much more on my plate, but none of it felt like a burden. Every moment felt intentional. Every word I wrote and every message I shared felt like it had meaning. I was not doing this because I had to; I was doing it because I wanted to serve God. That is when I realized what a calling truly is. It is not just about having a goal. It is about having a reason that stirs your heart and aligns with God's will. For the first time in my life, I was not chasing happiness. I was walking in fulfillment.

Jeremiah 29:11 became a cornerstone verse for me. It says, "For I know the plans I have for you," declares the Lord, "plans to prosper you and not to harm you, plans to give you hope and a future." That verse carries a promise that goes deeper than comfort. It is a declaration that God already has the path laid out for us, even when we cannot see it. The part that stands out most to me is that He says the plans are for our good. God does not make mistakes, and He does not set us up to fail.

I remember hearing one of my pastors preach on that verse one Sunday. It was as if he was speaking directly to me. I had been battling impostor syndrome with my ministry. Even though I felt called, I kept thinking, "Who am I to do this? Who am I to speak about God's Word? Who am I to lead others?" I was wrestling with the idea that maybe I was not ready, maybe I was not good enough, or maybe I was just pretending. Then, that pastor said something that completely changed my mindset. He said, "God does not call the equipped. He equips the called."

That sentence hit me like a wave. It was like God Himself was reminding me that my worth and ability were not defined by my resume, but by His will. If He was calling me to ministry, then He would also prepare me for everything that came with it. I did not have to have all the answers. I did not need to be perfect. I just needed to be willing.

That realization lifted a huge weight off my shoulders. It helped me see that my calling was not something I had to earn. It was something I had to accept. When we walk with God, He gives us what we need along the way. It is not about being ready. It is about being faithful.

Another thing I learned is that calling is not a destination, but a lifestyle. For me, a year ago, I rarely opened my Bible. I rarely prayed, and I certainly was not giving sermons or leading devotionals. But as my faith grew, so did my discipline. Now, I cannot go a day without spending time in the Word. I cannot go long without praying. My days feel incomplete without writing or preparing a message.

When God calls us, He also reshapes our lives to make room for that calling. I realized that I had to trade some things that used to take up my time for things that nourished my soul. The hours I used to spend on video games or television became hours spent reading, praying, or ministering. At first, it felt strange to let go of the habits I had clung to for years, but over time I found that I was not losing anything at all. I was gaining peace, joy, and a sense of purpose that I had never experienced before.

I knew that ministry was my calling, and I suspected that God would use it to help people. What I did not realize was how quickly He would begin doing that. One moment in particular stands out to me. I was at a cookout with some friends from a life group I attend, and I had been put in charge of the grill. It was one of those warm, casual evenings where the laughter flows easily and the smell of food fills the air. I was standing there flipping burgers, talking to a buddy of mine about life.

He began to open up about his relationship. He told me that his girlfriend was on a work contract that would eventually end, and when it did, she would have to decide whether to stay with him or move back home. It was a heavy situation, and I could see the stress written all over his face. I did what I try to do best: I listened. When he asked for advice, I told him something that came to me in the moment, something I believe God placed on my heart.

I said, "Even though we might have limited time to do something, we should not let that looming deadline stop us from enjoying the time God gave us."

To me, it felt like a simple observation, something anyone might say. But to him, it was exactly what he needed to hear. He thanked me afterward and said that I had given him a new way to look at his situation. I was floored. In my mind, I had just offered a few words in passing. To him, it was a message from God.

That moment reminded me that sometimes purpose is not found in grand actions, but in small conversations. Sometimes it is not about standing on a stage or speaking to a crowd. Sometimes it is just about showing up, listening, and letting the Holy Spirit speak through us.

I have also had moments where I have prayed over people and felt unsure if my words were making any difference. There are times when I have walked away wondering if what I said really mattered. Then, days or weeks later, I hear back from them, and they tell me that things have turned around, or that their pain is gone, or that they finally feel at peace. To me, it was just a short prayer. To them, it was life-changing.

It humbled me deeply, because it reminded me that none of this power is mine. I do not take credit for saying the right thing or for anyone's healing. That is God at work. The Holy Spirit gives me the words to say, and God listens to the prayers that we lift up. If it is His will, He brings healing and change. My part is simply to obey and trust that He knows what He is doing.

That is the beautiful thing about purpose. It is not about us being capable. It is about God being faithful.

I also began to see how God uses our past mistakes for His glory. I have made plenty of them, and for a long time I thought that my failures disqualified me from being used by God. But now, I see that the very things I once regretted have become tools that allow me to help others. In the youth ministry that I help lead, I often find myself talking to young men about lessons I learned the hard way.

I share with them how I used to bottle up my emotions, believing that showing them made me weak. I tell them how that mindset kept me from healing and how important it is to bring everything to God, even the feelings we do not understand. I talk to them about relationships, about communication, and about learning to trust God's timing. Every mistake I made became a teaching moment. Every failure became a story of grace. I want them to learn what took me years to discover.

That is what purpose looks like in motion. It is not about perfection, but about progress. God takes the broken pieces of our past and arranges them into something beautiful. He takes our weakness and makes it our strength.

Ultimately, I believe my career will be as a pastor. But my purpose goes deeper than a job title. My purpose is the same as a shepherd's. My purpose is to lead people home. Every message I write, every prayer I pray, every conversation I have is another step toward guiding someone closer to God.

I believe that God gave each of us tools long before we even knew what they were for. Some people have the gift of speaking. Some have the gift of listening. Some have the ability to serve quietly behind the scenes, and others have the heart to lead. Whatever the gift, it is meant for His glory. My calling is to use the tools He gave me, and I trust that as I keep walking forward, He will continue to equip me for whatever lies ahead.

There are still days when I doubt myself. There are still times when I wonder if I am doing enough or if I am doing it right. But even in those moments, I remind myself that God knows the plans He has for me. He knows where I am going, even when I do not. My responsibility is not to have the whole map. My responsibility is to take the next faithful step.

Purpose is not about knowing every detail of the journey. It is about trusting the One who leads you.

Every part of my story, from the struggles to the victories, has been shaping me into who I am today. God has used the moments that broke me to teach me compassion. He has used the seasons of silence to strengthen my faith. He has used every twist and turn to prepare me for where I am now.

I often tell people that their story matters. Even the parts that seem unimportant or messy are part of something greater. When we surrender our story to God, He weaves it into His plan for the world. The pain we thought was meaningless becomes someone else's hope. The lesson we learned in hardship becomes someone else's guide.

That is what I love most about living with purpose. It connects us to something eternal. It reminds us that our lives have meaning beyond what we see.

Every time I sit down to write or speak, I ask God to use my words for His kingdom. I pray that what I create does not just inspire, but transforms. I want the people who hear or read my messages to walk away with a sense of peace, to know that God has a plan for them too. Because He does.

If there is one thing I have learned, it is that purpose is not limited to the walls of a church or the reach of a ministry. It can be found in our workplaces, in our families, in every interaction we have. Every act of kindness, every encouraging word, and every quiet prayer is part of fulfilling that calling.

Your purpose does not have to look like mine. Maybe your calling is to raise a family in faith. Maybe it is to create art that speaks truth. Maybe it is to work in a field that brings light to others. Whatever it is, trust that God will equip you for it, just as He did for me.

I still do not have every tool I will need. I still make mistakes. But I know that as I continue to walk with God, He will shape me into exactly who I need to be. I no longer need to worry about controlling every outcome. I do not have to chase fulfillment. I have found it.

Because purpose is not about being perfect. It is about being willing. It is about saying yes when God calls and trusting that He knows what He is doing.

So now, when I ask myself, "What am I meant to do?" I already know the answer. I am meant to serve. I am meant to love. I am meant to lead people closer to the One who never stopped leading me.

My journey is still just beginning, but I walk it with confidence now. Because I know this truth: we may not know the path, but God always holds the map. And He will never lead us astray.

Conclusion – The Road Ahead

When I look back over the path that has brought me here, I see so many different versions of myself. There was the version who was lost, searching for meaning in things that could never satisfy. There was the version who thought strength meant hiding pain, and that success meant control. There was the version who ran from God, believing that He could not possibly use someone as flawed as me. And then, slowly, there was the version who began to stop running.

It started small. A few prayers whispered at night. A moment of honesty with myself about the things that were broken. A decision to start reading the Word again. Then it grew. I began to see that the same God who created the stars cared enough to meet me in my mess. I began to realize that my failures were not the end of my story, but the foundation of something new.

Each chapter of my life has carried a lesson that I needed to learn. In my struggles, I found humility. In my brokenness, I found grace. In my questions, I found faith. In my repentance, I found freedom. And through it all, I found love. I did not find those things on my own. They were given to me by a God who refused to give up on me, even when I had nearly given up on myself.

There were days when I felt like my life was standing still. Days when I wondered if I was making any difference at all. I think we all feel that way sometimes. We pray and do not hear an answer. We work and do not see results. We serve and do not receive recognition. In those moments, I have learned that God is still moving, even when I cannot see it. The silence is not His absence. It is often His preparation.

Philippians 1:6 has become one of the verses that anchors me in those seasons. It says, "He who began a good work in you will carry it on to completion until the day of Christ Jesus." That promise reminds me that God does not abandon the work He starts. Every seed He plants in our hearts will grow in its time. Every calling He places within us will unfold exactly as it should.

When I think about my journey, I see that truth everywhere. God began His good work in me long before I ever recognized it. He was shaping me through every joy and every trial. Even in the times when I felt furthest from Him, He was near, guiding me back.

The wandering had purpose. The pain had purpose. The waiting had purpose. Every step, every setback, every small victory was part of something bigger than I could understand.

Now, as I continue to walk forward, I do so with gratitude. I am grateful that God allowed me to fall, because it taught me to rely on Him. I am grateful for the nights when I cried out in confusion, because they reminded me of His comfort. I am grateful for the mistakes I made, because they showed me that His grace never runs dry.

If there is one thing I want every reader to take away from this journey, it is this: God is not finished with you. No matter where you are right now, no matter how far you feel from Him, He is still writing your story. The pages you regret are not wasted. The chapters you wish you could rewrite are the very ones He will use to reveal His glory.

I spent so long believing that purpose was something to be earned. That I had to fix myself before I could be worthy of God's love. But the truth is, God loved me before I ever took a step toward Him. He loves each of us in that same way. He sees the whole story, beginning to end, and still chooses to walk with us.

Faith is not about having every answer. It is about trusting the One who does.

As I have grown in my ministry, I have learned that faith is not a single moment, but a daily rhythm. Some days it feels effortless. Other days it feels like climbing a mountain. But even on the hardest days, I know that God is with me. Every time I doubt, He reminds me of the people who have been touched by something I said or wrote. Every time I question my ability, He reminds me that He is the one doing the work through me.

It amazes me how God uses even the smallest acts for His kingdom. A word spoken in kindness, a prayer whispered in secret, a moment of patience in a frustrating situation, all of it matters. The kingdom of God is built not just on miracles and grand gestures, but on everyday faithfulness.

I have learned to see the beauty in the ordinary. When I wake up in the morning and pray, I feel His presence in the quiet. When I write a devotional, I feel His hand guiding the words. When I share time with others, I see His love reflected in their faces. Purpose is not always loud. Sometimes it is as simple as being present where God has placed you.

There have been moments in my ministry when I felt like I was running on empty. I would look at my analytics and see only a handful of views. I would think to myself, "What am I doing wrong?" But then, every so often, I would receive a message from someone saying that a devotional helped them through a difficult time. That is when I am reminded that numbers do not measure impact. God measures hearts.

I once prayed that God would let me see how He was using my work. His answer was gentle but firm: "You are not meant to see it all. Trust Me." That taught me to stop chasing validation and start trusting obedience. My job is not to measure results. My job is to say yes.

And the more I said yes, the more I realized that my story is not really mine alone. It belongs to God. He took every broken piece and turned it into something meaningful. He used every wound as a place for His light to shine through. He turned my failures into testimonies, my weaknesses into lessons, and my fears into faith.

That is what God does for all of us.

Maybe your story feels unfinished. Maybe you are still searching for what comes next. I want you to know that is okay. You do not have to have it all figured out. None of us do. What matters is that you take the next step, even if it is small. Read a verse. Say a prayer. Ask God to reveal His plan in His time.

If you feel like you have wandered too far, remember that God is still calling your name. If you feel like you are too broken, remember that He specializes in rebuilding hearts. If you feel like you have failed too often, remember that His mercy is new every morning.

You are not disqualified. You are not forgotten. You are not alone.

Every season of life has its own purpose. Some are meant for learning. Some are meant for waiting. Some are meant for serving. And some are meant for simply resting in God's presence. Wherever you are right now, know that it is part of His plan.

When I think about the road ahead, I no longer see it as something to fear. I see it as something to walk with faith. I do not know every turn it will take, but I know who walks beside me. And that is enough.

I still dream about the future; about the people I will meet, the sermons I will give, the devotionals I will write, and the lives that may be touched through them. But more than that, I dream about staying faithful. I want my life to be a reflection of gratitude, a living testimony to the grace that saved me.

The same God who brought me here will bring me through everything that comes next. The same God who began this work in me will see it through to completion.

Maybe your story looks different from mine. Maybe you are just starting to ask questions about faith. Maybe you have been walking with God for years but feel distant now. Or maybe you are somewhere in between. Wherever you are, God is not done with you. He is writing your story one day at a time.

Take a moment and think about where you are right now in your journey. Think about what God has already done for you, even in ways you may not have noticed. Every breath you take is proof of His grace. Every sunrise is a reminder that His mercy never ends.

The beauty of faith is that it does not depend on how strong we are. It depends on how faithful God is. And He has never failed to be faithful.

As I close this chapter, I find myself filled with hope. Hope for what comes next in my life, and hope for what comes next in yours. I have learned that faith is not just about looking back at what God has done, but looking forward to what He will do.

We are all part of His story; a story that began before we were born and will continue long after we are gone. Each of us is a chapter in His book of redemption. And the Author never makes mistakes.

So wherever you are, keep walking. Keep believing. Keep trusting. Because the God who began a good work in you will carry it on until the day of completion.

That is His promise. And I am living proof that He keeps His promises.

Sometimes at night, I still find myself looking up at the moon. It's no longer a reminder of how small I am, but of how deeply I am known. The same light that once made me feel unseen now reminds me of the One who never lost sight of me. I don't see distance anymore; I see design. I don't see silence; I see grace. The same God who hung that moon in the sky is the same God who reached down to lift me out of my wandering. I used to see the moon and feel alone, now I see it and remember that I walk in His light. I remember that I'm not something that exists apart from Him, but a reflection of His light.

www.ingramcontent.com/pod-product-compliance
Lightning Source LLC
LaVergne TN
LVHW041225080426
835508LV00011B/1082